Alcatraz

Island of Change

by

JAMES P. DELGADO

photography by

ROY EISENHARDT

Contents

The Golden Gate National Park Association is a non-profit membership organization established to support the education, conservation and research programs of the Golden Gate National Recreation Area.

PUBLISHED BY
GOLDEN GATE NATIONAL
PARK ASSOCIATION

ISBN 0-9625206-6-7

Rising *from the cold, fast-moving waters of*
San Francisco Bay, an island's once barren slopes lie hidden beneath
crumbling brick and concrete buildings. For over a hundred years, this
island has been reworked and altered by human activity, first as a fort,
then as a military prison and a federal penitentiary. Early brick and
cut-stone buildings form the foundations of more modern structures
of reinforced concrete, creating a layer cake of history in the compact
space of a steep, 22-acre island. It is an historic place, its name known
throughout the world. It is Alcatraz Island.

Visitors to the island come to see remnants of the past.
Alcatraz is best known for its sinister reputation, one that has long
dominated the nation's consciousness. The most famous, if not the
most infamous, prison in the United States, Alcatraz and the men who
lived within its rockbound and tide-swept fastness inspired countless
tales, many set to print in books and articles, others on film. Called
"the Rock," "Hellcatraz," and "Uncle Sam's Devils Island," Alcatraz is
best remembered for its 29 years as the maximum-security, minimum-
privilege federal penitentiary that housed some of America's most
notorious criminals. Al Capone, George "Machine Gun" Kelly, Alvin
Karpis, Doc Barker, and Robert "Birdman" Stroud all spent time on
Alcatraz, and their notoriety added to the intense scrutiny afforded to
the island prison so close to San Francisco, yet a world away.

Today, Alcatraz is the only former federal penitentiary
open to the public, and is a favorite destination in the 75,000-acre
Golden Gate National Recreation Area. Each year, nearly a million
people visit the island, drawn by "the Rock's" reputation. They come
to see Alcatraz's cellhouse and crumbling ruins set against the spectac-
ular views of San Francisco, the Bay, and the Golden Gate. Yet the
stark walls and tiny cells of the prison and the compelling quality of

*the island's ruined and crumbling buildings offer only one part of
the Alcatraz story.*

There is another world to explore on this tiny island.

*In a manmade landscape left to deteriorate, the natural
world is taking the island back. The tall eucalyptus and cypress trees,
bent and shaped by the winds that sweep through the Golden Gate and
across the Bay, are bathed by the thick mists of fog that blanket the
island. Tangled carpets of grass, agave, mirror plant, blackberries,
and other plants cover walls, paths, and the broken piles of rubble that
mark the sites of correctional officer apartment houses on the parade
ground. Roses bloom in the overgrown wilderness of once-formal
gardens.*

*The natural world of Alcatraz, visible in the lush greenery
growing amid the ruins and the gulls which swoop and whirl over its
shores, tells another side of the island's story.*

*At the time of its "discovery" by European explorers,
Alcatraz was home to a major seabird colony. The birds, once dis-
placed by construction and human inhabitants, have now returned in
substantial numbers. Separated by more than a mile of water from the
mainland, the shores of Alcatraz provide protected nesting areas for
gulls, night-herons, and other roosting birds, offering them safety from
mainland predators like rats, raccoons, and dogs.*

*Even now, this natural part of the island remains a mys-
tery. Many visitors catch only a glimpse of it from the harbor tour
boats or the island's summit as they exit the cellhouse. But everyone
who comes to Alcatraz leaves with a sense of the place, of its isolation
in the midst of a bustling seaport, of its fate carved by the forces of
tides and currents, wind and fog, human endeavor and struggle for
life on the rock.*

*Out in the middle of the Bay, the island is a world unto
itself. Isolation, one of the constants of island life for any inhabitant--
soldier, prisoner, bird or plant—is a recurrent theme in the unfolding
history of Alcatraz.*

$

A Barren Rock

WEATHERED AND WORN, its face mottled with the dark green of sea moss and stained with lichens, Alcatraz Island rises from the current-swept waters near the Golden Gate.

Like other islands in the Bay, Alcatraz is a drowned mountain peak. A million years ago, San Francisco Bay was a broad valley interrupted by ridges and peaks. Rivers running west from the Sierra Nevada through this valley were eventually blocked by the rising mountains of the Coast Range. Thrust upward by shifting continental plates, the Coast Range ran unbroken along the Pacific's shores except at a small gorge that would one day be named the Golden Gate. Here, sixteen of the rivers from the Sierra Nevada converged to flow to the sea.

Melting icecaps first flooded the valley that would become San Francisco Bay 300,000 years ago. The invading ocean and primeval bay retreated during another ice age, until a warmer climate and glacial melting 10,000 years ago sent the rising sea into the valley once again. Entering through the gorge at the mouth of the great river that flowed through the valley, the waters nearly covered the peaks and ridges of the interior. The ocean stopped beyond the straits of Carquinez. There, the tremendous flow of water from the Sierra met the ocean.

Breaking the surface of the newly created bay, a small sandstone peak, thinly covered with soil, was smoothed and shaped by currents sweeping in and out with the tides through the Golden Gate. The soil clinging to the drowned flanks washed away, exposing the seamed, mottled blue-gray stone. This barren rock, rising before the Golden Gate, we know today as Alcatraz.

The bottom of the bay surrounding Alcatraz is a soft landscape of mud, some of it dozens of feet deep. The mud, formed from soil washed into the bay by rivers, has softened the contours of the valley that flooded 10,000 years ago. The original riverbed, running north of Alcatraz, is now a current-swept channel nearly 200 feet deep that lies between Alcatraz and Angel Island. The bottom slopes gradually, then rises sharply to form Alcatraz's shores. To the west of the island, a smaller peak rises, its tip barely washed by the tidal swell. This is Little Alcatraz, formerly known as "Paul Pry Rock," after an excursion steamer wrecked on it in the 1860s.

Where Alcatraz's steep slopes meet the water, the soft sandstone has crumbled before the ocean's onslaught. The western shore of Alcatraz is slowly eroding. Throughout the 1800s, military engineers shored the slopes and filled behind brick and concrete retaining walls in an effort to combat the relentless retreat of land. Alcatraz, however, continues to crumble. Small sea caves penetrate beneath the island, following the cracks and fissures of the rock.

The First People Arrive

The first people to see Alcatraz Island were Native Americans whose settlements dotted the Bay's shore nearly 3,000 years ago. These native peoples thrived on a rich harvest from the sea. In the reed-clogged shallows and estuaries, they fished, gathered shellfish, and hunted for waterfowl. From reeds, or tules, they wove thick bundles into gently arching canoes that navigated the Bay and ventured into the open Pacific as far as the distant, dim crags of the Farallon Islands, twenty-six miles west of the Golden Gate.

These ancient mariners roamed the Bay, stopping to hunt for birds' eggs on Alcatraz or perhaps fish from its shores. But the rocky slopes of Alcatraz, washed by fog and whipped by wind, offered no shelter or fresh water. Nearby Angel Island, thickly cloaked with trees and brush that flourished near freshwater springs, was the site of several settlements that provided easy access to Alcatraz.

Years later, the Spanish would be the first Europeans to see San Francisco Bay and give Alcatraz Island its name. Beginning in 1542, Spanish vessels sailed along the California coast and past the Golden Gate, but none ventured into the Bay. Abandoning plans for further exploration and settlement of California, the Spanish only returned to the coast in 1769 in response to rumors of Russian interest in claiming this far-flung outpost. The Spanish government sent a land party from San Diego to Monterey Bay, but the expedition bypassed its original destination and instead stumbled across San Francisco Bay.

Spanish soldiers scouting the Bay's shores in the years that followed spotted Alcatraz and the other islands, but it was not until 1775 that a European vessel entered the Bay through the Golden Gate.

On August 5 of that year, the small fregata, *San Carlos*, commanded by Juan Manuel de Ayala, sailed into the Bay and anchored off Angel Island. Setting out in the ship's small launch, the expedition's pilot, Jose Canizares, charted and named the prominent landmarks.

Canizares described an arid island, without a harbor, and populated by waterfowl. This he named *La Isla de los Alcatraces*, after the small *alcatraceo*, a cormorant native to northern Spain. Although later historians would claim the name for the Bay's pelicans, whose name in Spanish is *alcaraz*, the island was named Alcatrace, a name closer in fact to the term *alcatraceo*, for the cormorants whose sleek black bodies covered the guano-streaked island as they sunned themselves.

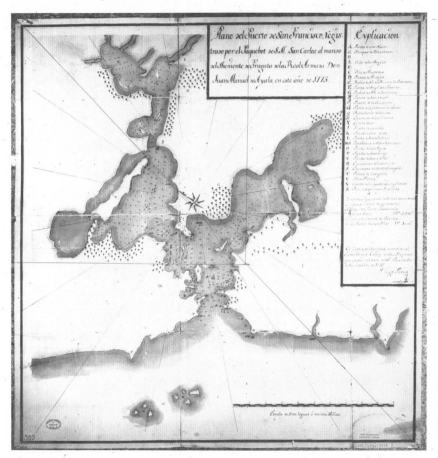

The Naming of Alcatraz

Scholars disagree about whether the Spanish explorers who first sailed into San Francisco Bay in 1775 actually named the tiny island that is known today as Alcatraz, or instead described larger Yerba Buena Island. The latter bore the name Isla de los Alcatraces on the first expedition's charts, but the description penned by expedition leader Juan Manuel de Ayala appears to better fit the island we now call Alcatraz: "tan arida y escarpada que ni para lanchas havia puerto a esta le puse de los Alcatraces por la abundancia que tiene de ellos." Translated, the island was "so barren and craggy that it could provide no shelter even for small craft and it was called the Alcatraces because of the large numbers of them that were there."

Transforming the Island

Blackberries are thick on Alcatraz.

The barren fastness of Alcatraz greeted the first people to inhabit the Bay Area. The island, lacking fresh water and open to the winds that swept in from the sea, was uninhabitable. But its rich and diverse marine life—from sea mammals to mussels and birds—brought people to Alcatraz's shores to gather food.

The first English written descriptions of Alcatraz were made by U.S. Army surveyors in 1847. They found only a thin crust of earth scarcely capable of supporting a few tufts of grass that sprouted from nooks in the rocks. In many ways, Alcatraz at that time was probably similar to Red Rock Island farther up the Bay, with its sparse growth of native grasses and plants.

During the next few decades, military engineers hauled soil from nearby Angel Island to Alcatraz. The soft earth, piled in front of gun emplacements, would absorb the impact of incoming shells. In this soil, the military tried and failed to grow grass, alfalfa, and clover, finally giving up in 1904 because of the lack of water. Hardier natives thrived on the island, however. Native plants now found on Alcatraz—coyote brush, California poppy, and blackberry—probably came to the island as seeds mixed in with the soil brought from Angel Island.

The dirt brought over to Alcatraz later supported gardens on the island's rocky slopes. Trees, shrubs, and bushes planted in 1853 provided shade and shelter as well as ornamentation on the barren rock. In the 1860s, deep pits were blasted and cut into the rock and filled with soil that may have introduced insects and rodents to Alcatraz.

Rosa cinnamomea.

Roses were cultivated in the formal gardens of Alcatraz. In the 1880s, well-tended gardens flourished in front of the old Army Citadel and elsewhere on the island.

On Alcatraz today, grasses, mosses, cypress, and brush cover the island, spilling over rock walls and clogging every crack in the pavement. The greenery softens the angular sandstone and mutes the island's sharp profile. Alcatraz is no longer a barren rock in the Bay.

As Alcatraz became the site of a fort and then a military prison, soldiers and their families living on the island continued to modify "the Rock." In 1885, a newspaper reporter described how each officer's home had a "little garden plot." These formal gardens in time overflowed their manmade boundaries. As more soil was imported, and when the batteries of the fort were buried as the island's use as a prison increased, vast expanses of Alcatraz gave way to plantings.

Excellent swimmers, deer mice may have arrived on Alcatraz by swimming across the Bay. Coming out at night to feed, these small, buff-colored mice eat insects, grains, seeds, and fruit. The mice, in turn, are hunted by gulls, kestrels, and ravens, which keep the mice from overrunning the tiny island.

In the early 1900s, the island fairly blossomed in spring and summer. On February 7, 1924, the California Spring Blossom and Wildflower Association planted hundreds of pine, sequoia, and cypress seedlings on Alcatraz along with wildflower seeds. Gradually, the rugged island was transformed, all part of a concerted effort by the military "to improve the rock itself so that its own beauty shall be in harmony with that of its surroundings," as one March 1918 account noted. "The visitor who comes here expects to find a barren rock, but as he strolls over it he is surprised to find roses in bloom, sweet peas, lilies and a large variety of other flowers in all their beauty and fragrance... In this way barren wastes are converted into garden spots, and ugliness is transformed into beauty."

$\int$

The Fort, Lighthouse and Military Prison

ROMANTIC LEGEND TELLS of Spanish dungeons carved into the rock of Alcatraz, but in fact no one lived on the tiny island during the decades that Spain, and then Mexico, ruled California. In the waning days of Mexican control in the 1840s, Governor Pio Pico granted Alcatraz to naturalized citizen Julian Workman of Los Angeles. The deed was signed on June 8, 1846, the eve of the United States' conquest of California. Pico's transfer of the island to Workman, who in turn conveyed it to his son-in-law Francis Temple, stipulated that the grantee establish a lighthouse on Alcatraz as soon as possible. But a war with Mexico and a new government intervened.

The discovery of gold in California in January 1848 brought hundreds of thousands of emigrants to the territory, and thousands of ships. By 1849, the village of San Francisco had blossomed into a major city of 20,000. The protection of San Francisco Bay and California became a high priority for the United States, second only to the defense of New York City and its great port.

The Army Comes to the Rock

The importance of San Francisco Bay, by now the principal American harbor on the Pacific, and the proximity of Alcatraz Island to the Golden Gate, made the island an excellent site for seacoast defenses. Military officer and explorer John Charles Fremont, the man who named the Golden Gate, described the island soon after the U.S. conquest of California as "the best position for Lighthouse and Fortifications in the Bay of San Francisco." U.S. Topographical Engineers attached to the occupying Army surveyed Alcatraz in May 1847. They found only a barren rock capable of supporting little life.

Following the United States' annexation of California at the end of the Mexican War in 1848, a board of Army and Navy officers convened to decide how best to protect the prized port. They declared Alcatraz Island the perfect site for batteries of cannon. To defend San Francisco harbor, military engineers envisioned two massive brick forts at the Golden Gate, a third fort on Alcatraz, and smaller batteries at

Fort Mason (Point San Jose), Angel, and Yerba Buena islands. These fortifications placed enemy vessels within reach of U.S. guns from Mile Rock to Telegraph Hill and Rincon Point (now the San Francisco anchorage of the Bay Bridge).

President Millard Fillmore, acting on his officers' recommendations, proclaimed vast tracts of land in San Francisco, Marin, and Alcatraz, Angel, Yerba Buena, and Mare islands as military reservations on November 6, 1850. To oversee the construction of fortifications, the Army created a "Board of Engineers for the Pacific Coast" in 1851. The engineers surveyed Alcatraz in the summer of 1852, and within a year work began. Laborers blasted, chipped, and hauled stone and laid brick for the first emplacements on the island's shores. Between 1854 and 1859, blasting transformed its rocky slopes into platforms for massive cast-iron cannon. Manned in late 1859, Alcatraz's guns were part of the first permanent U.S. fortifications on the Pacific coast.

The earliest plans for fortifying Alcatraz called for 68 smoothbore cannon, but the outbreak of the Civil War in 1861 hastened the construction of additional emplacements. At that time, gold-rich San Francisco had grown into the 12th-largest urban center in the country and was the heart of an industrial and agricultural empire on the Pacific. As the importance of defending the Golden Gate increased with rising national and international tension, platforms for 155 guns

Alcatraz Shipwrecks
Over the years, ships navigating the unpredictable waters of San Francisco Bay have hit, stranded or were wrecked on Alcatraz. The first known casualty was the ship Arkansas, *which went ashore on Alcatraz after arriving at San Francisco on December 19, 1849, fully loaded with passengers and cargo bound for the gold fields.*
A 330-ton excursion steamer, the Paul Pry, *hit Little Alcatraz Island and sank during a tour of the Bay's defenses on December 22, 1862, earning the islet the name "Paul Pry Rock." The* Oliver Cutts *wrecked on Little Alcatraz on January 13, 1868. Only the mizzenmast was visible, left, when Eadweard Muybridge photographed it several months later.*

ringed Alcatraz's shores. By the end of 1865, Alcatraz's engineers reported that the island's guns could simultaneously discharge a barrage of 6,949 pounds of shot.

Life for soldiers on the barren rock was difficult. Isolated from the mainland by more than a mile of water, the resident engineers and soldiers had to rely on the regular transport steamer to get to San Francisco. More adventuresome souls rowed to town. Wells could not be dug, and while cisterns blasted out of the rock captured rain water, fresh water had to be shipped over by barge, along with all provisions. A garden was planted on nearby Angel Island to grow food.

Second Lieutenant James Birdeye McPherson, arriving at Alcatraz in late 1857 to oversee the construction of fortifications, complained in his letters of the fierce winds that swept the rock each day, the "never ceasing roar of the breakers dashing against the rocks," and the boredom of his isolation. Every weekend, and "when I get tired of playing the hermit," McPherson rowed to town but "I get a good wetting about every third time I go over."

The officers who garrisoned the post after 1859 brought their families to the island. Wives and children helped brighten the social horizons as well as the island itself. The new residents planted trees and grew flower and vegetable gardens, alleviating the harshness of the rock. Still, these inhabitants, as would all others, had to cope with the isolation of life on an island in the midst of a busy harbor on the Pacific coast.

Fortifying Alcatraz: The Fort

The Army's fortifications included open-air batteries to mount 6-, 8-, and 10-inch Columbiad cannon on wooden carriages that pivoted to rotate on railed platforms. The first guns, mounted to face San Francisco in April 1855, were seven-and-a-half-ton, 10-inch Columbiads named for the bore of the gun and the diameter of their shot. More modern weapons were eventually placed on Alcatraz, including the largest practical cannon of the Civil War era, the 15-inch Rodman. This hefty cannon's 440-pound shot could fly three miles and tear through thick oak planks or an ironclad's metal hull. Three of these 50,000-pound behemoths were installed on Alcatraz—the first on July 20, 1864. Along with the guns, the Army also fortified the island with tall brick defensive walls and a thick-walled "sallyport," complete with moat, drawbridge and two casemated embrasures for 24-pound flank howitzers. The guns could spray the road with shot and shrapnel to prevent an enemy's easy access up the slopes.

A casemated brick barracks at the wharf and a massive defensive barracks, known as the Citadel, were also built. A moat surrounded the Citadel, which perched atop the island. The two-foot thick brick walls were pierced by narrow slits through which soldiers could

Built in the 1860s, the casemated brick barracks still stand near the island's wharf.

6/6 Arsenal & Ordnance Yard Alcatraz Island

Famed 19th-century photographer Eadweard Muy-bridge captured this post-Civil War view of the fortress on Alcatraz, top. The first guns mounted on Alcatraz were 8-inch Columbiad cannon, center. Following the war, the heavily fortressed island became a military prison. To house prisoners, a three-story concrete cell-house was built on top of the old Citadel at the island's summit in the early 1900s.

aim their carbines and rifles. Two stories tall, with a basement at the moat level, the Citadel was accessible only by drawbridge, had its own water supply, magazines, and storerooms and was designed to last out a protracted siege. It was the last line of defense on the island.

Civil War Tensions

Alcatraz Island, rising precipitously from the Bay in the front of their city, was foremost in the thoughts of most 19th-century San Franciscans. The military might of the fort on Alcatraz served as a reminder during the Civil War years, from 1861 to 1865, that the United States intended to hold and keep California, its 31st state, despite the vast, unsettled distances between the coasts. In a time of national disunion, the importance of California's gold, financial control of Nevada silver mines, mercury mines, grain, lumber, and its greatest asset, the port of San Francisco, were national priorities. The guns on Alcatraz stood ready to defend against any invading ships, be they Confederate raiders or British or French warships sympathetic to the Confederate cause.

Alcatraz's cannons actually barked once in anger. On October 1, 1863, an unidentified warship sailed through the Golden Gate and failed to answer Alcatraz's hail, so a shot was sent across the intruder's bow. The warship heaved to and fired a 21-gun salute. Much to the chagrin of the military, it turned out to be *HMS Sutlej*, flying the flag of Admiral John Kingcombe, commander of Her Majesty's Naval Forces in the Pacific. While an apology was offered to the British, a certain pride must have stirred the martial heart of the Army's Commanding General of the Department of the Pacific at the readiness and alertness of the troops on Alcatraz.

Civil War Lockup

The passions of the Civil War introduced a new use for Alcatraz. In August 1861, the military post on the island became a military prison. While its status as the most heavily defended federal outpost influenced the decision, the post's isolation in the Bay made it an ideal prison.

For the next thirty years, Alcatraz served a dual role as guardian of the Golden Gate and as a symbol of harsh military justice. Among the first prisoners were Army and Navy officers who refused to swear an oath of allegiance to the federal government after the southern states seceded. These men were followed by those who spoke in favor of the Confederacy, or who wanted California as a separate, pro-southern Pacific republic.

Military authorities arrested dozens of civilians, some of them prominent men and politicians, after President Abraham Lincoln suspended the writ of habeas corpus. For crimes ranging from speeches denouncing the military or the government to drunken toasts

Lighthouses on Alcatraz

Alcatraz Light:
Position: lat. 37°49'28"
N, long. 122°25'21" W
Height of Tower: 84 feet
Height of Focal Plane:
214 feet
Characteristic and Color:
Five-second white flash
(rotating beacon)
Daymark: Tower is
painted white.

The U.S. Government first made plans to build lighthouses on the Pacific coast in 1848, starting with Cape Disappointment at the mouth of Oregon's Columbia River. The end of the Mexican War that year and the annexation of California made San Francisco Bay the first priority for a lighthouse. The discovery of gold in California brought thousands of ships to San Francisco Bay in 1849 and 1850 and gave even more urgency to the need to light the Bay's approaches. In 1850, Congress voted its first appropriation for Pacific lighthouses. In 1852, work began on eight beacons along the California and Oregon coasts. The first two were for San Francisco—one at the Golden Gate itself at Fort Point, the other on Alcatraz.

The materials for the Alcatraz light arrived in the hold of the ship Tropic of New York on December 4, 1852. The foundation of the lighthouse was laid on the island's summit on December 15, and six months later, on June 21, 1853, the completed structure stood ready to mount its lamp and lens. The lighthouse was a 40-foot tall, one-and-a-half-story brick building sur-mounted by a short 8-foot diameter tower that cost $15,000 to build. It mounted a third-order Fresnel lens manufactured in France by L. Sauttier and Co. of Paris and shipped to the Pacific in the summer of 1853. On June 1, 1854, the light on Alcatraz shone out over the Bay for first time. From an elevation of 166 feet above the water, the light could be seen 14 miles out to sea. It was the first American lighthouse on the Pacific coast.

A keeper and assistant keeper were posted at the lighthouse by the newly created U.S. Lighthouse Board. The first keeper was Michael Cassin, who earned $750 a year by lighting the lamp every evening, cleaning the lens and glass in the tower, polishing the brass, keeping the oil lamps filled with the two quarts of sperm whale oil it burned each night, trimming the wicks, and maintaining the lighthouse. Keepers stayed with the lighthouse, bringing their families with them, until its operation was automated on November 14, 1963.

The Pacific coast's first lighthouse was torn down in 1909 when the top of Alcatraz Island was remodeled to accommodate the prison cellhouse. A new, 84-foot high reinforced-concrete lighthouse loomed over the cellhouse when it was lit for the first time on December 1, 1909. Quarters for the keepers were built at its base. A smaller lens—a fourth-order Fresnel—replaced the original third-order Fresnel.

Powered by electricity, the light on Alcatraz flashed out across the Bay and beyond the Golden Gate for as far as 19 miles. Built at a cost of $35,000, the "new" lighthouse was repowered in 1963 with a double-drum reflecting light, and the Fresnel lens, the last reminder of the 19th century, was removed.

The light on Alcatraz has remained lit for over 135 years, its service interrupted only once, when fire destroyed the keeper's quarters and disrupted power to the lighthouse on June 2, 1970. Relit with a small generator by the island's Native American occupiers, the beacon was permanently returned to duty by the Coast Guard on June 14. The flashing white light of Alcatraz, sweeping across the horizon from the darkened island every five seconds, dominates the center of the Bay each evening.

The Fog Signals
Alcatraz, a natural obstacle in an often fog-shrouded Bay, was marked with fog signals as well as a lighthouse. The first signal, built in 1856, was a massive 1,000-pound bell that was struck four times in a row by a clock-wound, 30-pound hammer every ten seconds in foggy weather.

In 1858, a newspaper reporter for the Daily Alta California described the bell's "clear, sonorous tone," noting it took three-and-a-quarter hours to wind down. The striking mechanism then had to be rewound, which took an hour or more of rapid work. "The bellman oftimes presses into service a merry party to help him with his labors, which are as arduous as those of a bone fide 'chain gang,' for four thousand revolutions are required to wind up the chain."

The original fog bell stood at the southeastern end of the island. In 1900, a second bell was added at the northwest end of Alcatraz. Replaced with sirens by 1915, the signals had new horns installed in 1961. The fog signals remain, but today deafening blasts from air horns fill the air.

to Jefferson Davis, President of the Confederate States, men were taken in hand and shipped to Alcatraz. There they were confined in the island's guardhouse, and later in a makeshift prison.

On Alcatraz, military prisoners had the "treason sweated out of them" as they broke rock and shoveled sand, with 24-pound iron balls chained to their legs. The men confined to Alcatraz included a group who had fitted out the schooner *J.M. Chapman* as a Confederate privateer. Loose talk and drunken waterfront gossip let the secret out, and when the *Chapman* sailed in March 1863, the Navy intercepted the hapless schooner. Towed to Alcatraz, the *Chapman* disgorged 15 prisoners, two brass cannon and ammunition.

The last of the Civil War prisoners taken to Alcatraz were 39 men arrested for the crime of being "so utterly infamous as to exult over the assassination of the President" in April 1865.

The island's use as a prison set a pattern that in time dominated Alcatraz. After the war, soldiers convicted of offenses ranging from desertion to murder served time on Alcatraz. Indians captured by the Army were also held on Alcatraz, including some of Geronimo's lieutenants, Hopi Indians, and Modoc Indians whose death sentences were commuted in the aftermath of the murder of a peace treaty party during California's Modoc War.

Successful as an island prison, Alcatraz was obsolete as an island fortress, despite efforts to modernize the defenses that continued through the 1870s. Changing technology doomed the brick-and-stone fortifications on Alcatraz. This fact was underscored on July 3, 1876, when the harbor defenses of San Francisco opened fire on a scow schooner moored as a target on the Bay during a great "Sham Battle" celebrating the nation's hundredth birthday. Alcatraz, Fort Point, and Marin County batteries fired without effect. Finally, an officer was dispatched in a boat to set fire to the unscathed target. When a female observer in the crowd swooned at his bravery, a Civil War veteran standing nearby rejoined, "Madam, with shooting like that, he's in the safest place in town."

"Uncle Sam's Devil's Island"

By 1898, a massive influx of prisoners from the Spanish-American War filled the prison's cells. The Army built a large wooden stockade to house the overflow. Plans for a major military prison on Alcatraz were drafted in the first decade of the 20th century, and in 1907, the last regular army troops garrisoning Alcatraz departed, replaced by soldiers from the U.S. Military Guard. Alcatraz became the "United States Military Prison, Pacific Branch," and between 1909 and 1912, a three-story reinforced concrete cellhouse, still standing today, was built at the island's summit. Woodframe and brick buildings were torn down or, in some cases, would later be used as the foundations of future concrete structures, like Building 64, which now looms over the

Rubble from the dismantled apartment houses litters the parade grounds in this view of the lighthouse and ruins of the old warden's house.

Alcatraz today bears little resemblance to the days of the fortress and military prison. The New Industries Building from the federal penitentiary era sits empty and off limits, ravaged by time, vandals and the island's corrosive climate. Little remains of the building that housed the laundry and workshops where prisoners built furniture and made World War II khakis, fatigues and cargo nets.

island's dock. The buttressed brick walls of batteries stripped of cannon were buried in rubble to form the open space of the parade ground at the island's southern end. Others were demolished and cast into the ocean.

As the dark brick of the island's batteries gave way to the stark concrete of prison buildings, Alcatraz began to attract considerable public attention. Soldiers still garrisoned the island and drilled, but now they guarded other soldiers, not the Golden Gate. Families of officers still lived in quaint Victorian houses lining the road leading to the island's summit, attended balls and receptions and entertained visitors. But this aspect of island life was lost in the shadow of the military prison.

Opposition to the prison arose in San Francisco, even among the ranks of the military. In 1913, no less a person than the Judge Advocate General of the U.S. Army, Major General Enoch H. Crowder, wrote that Alcatraz rose directly in the path of seaborne commerce that daily passed through the busy port; "its prominence in the harbor advertises, in a way unfair to the military service, the discipline of the Army…"

External criticism of the prison surfaced after 1918. In 1920, author Winthrop D. Lane, writing in *Survey* magazine, said that "the island is a death-house for the hopes and ambitions of many whose mistakes or misconduct have sent them there." Lane criticized the rules governing the prisoners as "numerous and rigid enough to cause constant annoyance and irritation," designed for the "actual repression of the men." Lane's article was the genesis of the idea that Alcatraz's isolation and discipline wore men down psychologically and broke their spirits.

THE ARMY RECLASSIFIED Alcatraz as a "Disciplinary Barracks" in 1915 to emphasize a program of rehabilitation, but the move had little effect on the negative talk circulating in San Francisco about the prison on the island. Rumors of sadistic treatment, moldering dungeons and a rock honeycombed with tunnels and secret passages continually surfaced. After a prisoner's successful escape from the island in 1923, *San Francisco Chronicle* reporter John L. Considine coined a new name for Alcatraz: "Uncle Sam's Devil's Island." The name stuck. When plans to locate a federal penitentiary on the island were announced in 1933, an article in the *Literary Digest* noted that the news brought "Devil's Island" back to the headlines.

Today, some of the fortifications that once dominated the island are visible as a stone-and-brick wall protruding from a cliff, the rounded brick foundation in the basement of the Model Industries Building, and part of the basement wall of the burned-out shell of the warden's house.

Water on the Rock

Alcatraz has no fresh water. To survive on the island, residents had to trap rain water in cisterns or bring it from the mainland. In 1854, Army engineers built a 23,000-gallon wooden watertank near the wharf. When the defensive barracks, or Citadel, was built atop the island's summit in 1858–1859, its roof was designed to catch rainwater and store it in 54,000-gallon brick cisterns on the building's southeast side.

Despite the cisterns, the Army quarter-master in 1862 reported that Alcatraz had insufficient water for the troops, and asked for a 182,000-gallon reservoir. Alcatraz's water system was augmented to a capacity of 175,000 gallons by the construction of more cisterns.

In 1868, the quartermaster spent $11,059 to ship 1,064,000 gallons of water to the rock. A pipe from the wharf was laid so that the steamers bringing water to Alcatraz could use their pumps to force the water up the hill and into the cisterns. By 1889, the enlarged cisterns held 241,543 gallons, or enough water to supply a 500-person garrison for eight months. It still was not enough, however, and in 1903, three large wooden water tanks were built atop the Citadel.

The Army drilled a well 300 feet into the island's rock between 1912 and 1913, but the water was salty and the well was abandoned. In 1910, the Army acquired a boat, the Aquador, for the run to Alcatraz. At the end of its tenure, the Army blasted two more cisterns into the rock at the northwest end of the island. These 250,000-gallon receptacles were augmented by six tanks holding 100,000 gallons atop the cellhouse. In 1939–1940, the Bureau of Prisons built the welded-steel water tank that dominates Alcatraz's skyline.

$\int$

The Federal Penitentiary

THE ARMY'S DISCONTENT WITH ALCATRAZ'S already darkened reputation and the high costs of maintaining the military prison prompted an announcement in 1933 that they would soon close it. The Department of Justice focused its attention on the rock, urged on by FBI Director J. Edgar Hoover who wanted a "super-prison" to house the criminals and public enemies being captured by his agents. On October 12, 1933, the Department of Justice signed a permit and acquired the island and its buildings, as well as 32 of the Army's "worst-case" prisoners. As the military left, personnel from the U.S. Bureau of Prisons set to renovating the Army's 1912 cellhouse and strengthening the island's security with chain-link fences, barbed wire, tool-proof steel bars, and guard towers. On July 1, 1934, Warden James A. Johnston formally opened the United States Penitentiary, Alcatraz.

The unique social circumstances of the 1930s, the notoriety of a number of its "guests," and a government web of secrecy about the prison and its operations guaranteed a media spotlight on Alcatraz. A nationwide crime wave in response to Prohibition and the Great Depression blasted its way into America's consciousness. "Public enemies" like "Baby Face" Nelson, "Machine Gun" Kelly, John Dillinger, Bonnie Parker and Clyde Barrow, the Ma Barker gang, and a host of other bank robbers, kidnappers, thugs, and murderers became well known, some attracting a following of readers who viewed them as modern-day Robin Hoods. The bloody campaign by the FBI to rid the country of these criminals attracted an equal amount of attention and increased the popularity of the "G-Men." In the FBI, America found a super police force to deal with gangsters who drove fast cars and outgunned small-town sheriffs and police. Dillinger, Ma Barker, and Bonnie and Clyde all met their ends in a hail of bullets. Other imprisoned public enemies, however, deserved a special fate—a super prison with a grim reputation. Alcatraz became just that place.

The public's fascination with America's badmen focused attention on the new penitentiary. In January 1934, six months before the new prison opened, the *San Francisco Chronicle* reported that

Al "Scarface" Capone, "Machine Gun" Kelly, and Harvey Bailey would be among the first prisoners to occupy cells on Alcatraz. Silence from the warden then, and in every other instance when called upon to confirm or deny inmate arrivals and identities, added to the air of mystery that shrouded the island penitentiary. The press was rarely invited to Alcatraz during its years of operation under the Bureau of Prisons. Reporters, like the rest of the world, had to make do with occasional press releases and telephoto views of the island. The lack of information from the Bureau of Prisons focused more attention on Alcatraz than an "open door" press policy. Dim, dreaded, mysterious, and vaguely sinister, "the Rock" was a deterrent to criminals both inside the federal prison system and in the outside world.

If the fame of some inmates and the silence of prison officials focused attention on Alcatraz, the lurid tales that occasionally escaped from the island's ring of secrecy had a profound impact on the nation. In the spring of 1935, inmate Verrill Rapp was paroled. Speaking to newspaper reporters, Rapp intimated that he and the other inmates suffered from "inhuman treatment."

In July 1935, another paroled Alcatraz con, William Henry Ambrose, told reporters about the psychological torment of being an Alcatraz inmate, invoking Warden Johnston's adherence to a rule of silence in the prison. In an interview in the *San Francisco Chronicle*, Ambrose said that "Capone is burning up at the restrictions....He's been in the hole (solitary) three or four times for talking. The 'no talk' rule is the hardest thing in Alcatraz life, for him, for every prisoner there." Ambrose lamented, "Not a word can be spoken by any of the convicts in line, at the table, at work, or in their cells...It's the toughest pen I've ever seen. The hopelessness of it gets to you. Capone feels it. Everyone does."

In February 1936, another released convict, Alfred Loomis, continued the litany of complaints, noting "they never give a guy a break." In 1937, the newspapers were full of Alcatraz news. In July, robber, kidnapper, and murderer Rufe Persful took an axe and chopped off the fingers of his left hand. In November, murderer Edgar Wutke slashed open his jugular vein with a pencil sharpener blade and bled to death. Their acts, if not inspired by a "hopeless" prison, were considered by the press and public as sure signs of Alcatraz's pernicious influence on its inhabitants. The public's opinion was reinforced by additional tales from released inmates, including Bryan Conway, who published his story in the *Saturday Evening Post* in February 1938. Mail-robber Roy Gardner published a sensational book, *Hellcatraz: The Rock of Despair*, and gave public lectures from nearby Treasure Island during the 1939 World's Fair in which he described an island "of the living dead." Even non-inmates got into the act. In September 1938, Anthony Turano, in an article headlined "America's Torture Chamber," in the *American Mercury* magazine, painted a grim picture of psycho-

Television and Alcatraz
Television has also used "the Rock" as a location, including a documentary-drama, "Alcatraz: The Whole Shocking Story," "Six Against the Rock," "Simon and Simon," "Midnight Caller," "Unsolved Mysteries," and a few episodes of "The Streets of San Francisco."

HAROLD HECHT PRESENTS
BURT LANCASTER BIRD MAN OF ALCATRAZ
featuring
KARL MALDEN / THELMA RITTER / NEVILLE BRAND / EDMOND O'BRIEN
A NORMA PRODUCTION UNITED ARTISTS

Hollywood and Alcatraz

Alcatraz fascinated Hollywood from its inception. Among the fictional tales and 'true-life' sagas that appeared on the silver screen during the '40s and '50s are King of Alcatraz, House Across the Bay, *and* Alcatraz Island. *Perhaps the best-known movie is the 1962 film,* The Birdman of Alcatraz, *starring Burt Lancaster as Robert 'Birdman' Stroud, who, ironically, never kept birds while imprisoned on the island.*

Other post-prison films that have used the island as a setting include Point Blank, The Enforcer—*a Dirty Harry offering, and perhaps the most well-known Alcatraz movie, the Clint Eastwood production* Escape from Alcatraz.

logical torture that included the island's proximity to San Francisco. "The barbarous effect is the same as chaining a starving man to a wall and spreading a feast beyond his reach."

Trials of inmates for escape attempts, assault and prison murders kept the papers full of news of Alcatraz. Not all the press was negative; a November 1935 story in the *Saturday Evening Post*, titled "The Rock," followed a fictional inmate's adjustment to the penitentiary. The article noted the use of metal detection devices and push-button tear gas dispensers in the "scientific stir," along with hand-picked guards trained in "target practice, scientific frisking, jujitsu and reading codes. They're as hard boiled as G-men." The penitentiary, in the words of the *San Francisco Examiner* in May 1936, "hurts, but it works."

For most Americans, Alcatraz became the epitome of the "tough" prison. Alcatraz was designed not just for public enemies, but for the most dangerous, notorious, and recalcitrant wards of the federal prison system. Alcatraz offered little in the way of rehabilitation. The inmates served hard time with limited privileges. As the regulations stated, "You are entitled to food, clothing, shelter and medical attention. Anything else you get is a privilege." Prison regulations were rigidly enforced, and violations were swiftly punished. Minor infractions brought a warning, while more serious offenses meant losing "good time," reduced privileges, or lock up in segregation—so-called "solitary confinement."

Violent crimes in the prison often brought rough handling. Punishment usually meant incarceration in the special treatment unit's isolation cells with bare steel walls, a blanket and pitch darkness when the lights were out. The last stop in the prison system, Alcatraz housed, in the eyes of many, the rottenest of the rotten apples.

Escape from Alcatraz

While inmates successfully escaped from the military prison on Alcatraz, no one made it off the island alive or without recapture during its 29-year federal penitentiary era. In all, prisoners made eight foiled and six partially successful escape attempts.

Sensational headlines followed an escape attempt on May 23, 1938. Three convicts beat Officer Royal Cline to death with a claw hammer and were stopped by the quick action of Officer Harold P. Stites, who ended the escape attempt by shooting two of the three when they assaulted his rooftop guard tower.

In May 1946, as six inmates attempted to "blast out" of Alcatraz with weapons seized from captured correctional officers, tens of thousands crowded the Bay's shore to watch U.S. Marines bombard the cellhouse with rifle grenades. Police launches, Coast Guard cutters

and launches circled the island while the battle raged to retake the prison. Three inmates and two correctional officers died, and several other officers were seriously injured. The trial of the three surviving inmate "ringleaders" emblazoned Alcatraz's name across America's newspaper headlines. Two of the three survivors were later executed at San Quentin for their role in the death of the officers.

The most famous escape, on June 11, 1962, is immortalized in the book and movie *Escape from Alcatraz*. Three inmates, including the leader, Frank Morris, chipped out of their cells, climbed to the top of the cellhouse, and then slipped off the island and into the Bay. They were never captured. Because personal effects were found floating in the Bay along with some of the makeshift equipment used in the escape, most authorities believe that the men drowned.

Hellcatraz

Alcatraz may have been an island of despair, but most of the time, life in the United States Penitentiary, Alcatraz, was no better or worse than that in most other prisons. A rigid set of regulations ruled the lives of the inmates; each man upon entering the institution received a set of regulations that governed his conduct, appearance, and scheduled his daily activities. The rules were not capricious and those that did not work, such as the early rule of silence, were withdrawn.

The prison's living conditions were good. Each man had a cell of his own. There was no overcrowding, and the cellhouse was kept neat and heated to a comfortable 70 degrees. After the mid-1950s, the well-lit cells were each equipped with a headset to tune in radio programs that were monitored and edited by prison officials. The inmates were kept clean and neat, with bedding and clothing frequently exchanged and laundered. Most inmates considered the meals good and plentiful. Pragmatic prison officials realized that good food was an incentive for good behavior.

The prison population averaged little more than 250 men, with five officers for each inmate as the general rule to help assure control. In all, Alcatraz housed just 1,576 inmates during its 29 years as a federal penitentiary. Each year witnessed a turn-around of approximately one-quarter of the inmate population as convicts were released or transferred to other, lower security institutions. Transfer to Alcatraz was not always a one-way trip to the end of the line.

As for its reputation as a psychological torture chamber, Alcatraz was not the "tomb of the living dead" that Roy Gardner once claimed. In 1949, recently retired warden James Johnston published *Alcatraz Island Prison and the Men Who Live There*. Johnston claimed remarkably good mental health among his former charges, noting that only one inmate, Wutke, committed suicide during his tenure as warden between 1934 and 1948, and that "fewer prisoners become psychotic in this prison than in other federal prisons." The ex-warden was in large measure correct. Recent research shows that incidents of mental illness at Alcatraz were no different from other prisons, notably U.S. Penitentiary, Leavenworth.

Indeed, some inmates chose Alcatraz as a place of confinement, either for protection in the maximum security environment from enforcers, or to relish the unique convict status of being bad enough to be sent to "the Rock." Alcatraz was considered by many to be one of the better prisons in which they served time. When the penitentiary closed in 1963—a victim of rising costs and deteriorating buildings—a *Newsweek* article quoted Associate Prison Director Fred T. Wilkenson, who described the departing cons as "softies." "Despite what they'd tell you, I think that they're going to miss this place." The words supposedly uttered by a departing inmate, however, better fit the popular image of the prison: "Alcatraz was no good for nobody."

Home on the Rock

Inmates weren't the only inhabitants of Alcatraz during the federal prison years. Many of the correctional officers and their families called the island home. Living in apartments in the converted military barracks that overlooked the dock, and later in reinforced concrete three-story apartment buildings on the parade ground, the residents of Alcatraz formed a close-knit island community. A volunteer fire department, social clubs and special holiday events flourished in the shadow of the prison atop the island.

Contact with inmates was limited, except for gardeners and other work crews. The gardens, planted and kept up by soldiers and their families, were later maintained by the prison. Inmate crews tended the flower beds, mowed the few patches of lawn, pruned the trees and planted flowers and bushes on the slopes below the cellhouse.

United States Penitentiary

Alcatraz, California

For most correctional officers and their families, the years on Alcatraz were the best years of their lives. Despite the tensions of crowded living, many formed close friendships in this beautiful setting in the middle of scenic San Francisco Bay. A regular newsletter, the *Fog Horn*, was published each month. Birthdays, personnel changes and promotions, articles about the island's social clubs and institutional news filled the mimeographed pages. Many of the officers felt safer living on Alcatraz than in San Francisco. They didn't have to worry about traffic, burglaries or violent crime. In the security of their isolated island, protected by fences and guard towers, few, if any, in the family quarters locked their doors at night. The only problems were isolation, a prohibition on pets, and the need to bring everything—from food to household furniture—to and from the island by boat. Children attended schools on the mainland and commuted to San Francisco with working mothers in the prison launch. The prison boat, at first an Army steamer that connected Alcatraz and Angel islands with Fort Mason on the mainland, and in time, the prison's own launch, *Warden Johnston*, made the 12-minute trip back and forth across the Bay. It carried commuting officers to work, ferried women and children from the island to San Francisco for school, jobs or for shopping trips, and transferred the occasional inmate to and from the island.

Even now, decades after the prison closed, former staff members and their children meet annually at reunions sponsored by the Alcatraz Alumni Association.

Closing the Prison

Ironically, the same reasons that led to the Army's departure from Alcatraz ultimately brought the Bureau of Prisons to the same conclusion. The prison had always faced substantial opposition, even from within the ranks of the Department of Justice. A rumor that the penitentiary would close within a year persisted for decades. In 1938, Attorney General Frank Murphy announced that Alcatraz was a place "conducive to a psychology that builds up a sinister and vicious attitude among the prisoners."

Pressure to close Alcatraz came as the costs of maintaining the prison rose higher and higher. The nearly century-old structures took constant upkeep, the 1912 cellhouse was crumbling, and the plumbing system was plagued by salt water that corroded pipes. The high costs of shipping everything to the island—fuel oil, food, even water itself—combined with the expense of guarding and feeding the prisoners to make this the most expensive upkeep in the nation.

A $5-million repair bill, and two embarrassing escapes in 1962, finally ended the island's nearly three-decade career as a federal prison. Attorney General Robert Kennedy closed Alcatraz on March 21, 1963. When the remaining 27 prisoners departed, leaving behind 336 empty cells, the last prisoner, Frank Weatherman, Alcatraz Number 1576, said "it's mighty good to get up and leave." A century after the first men were imprisoned on its shores, Alcatraz was no longer an island prison.

	A. M.		Leave Fort Mason		P. M.							A. M.
Week-Day	6:50*..	7:30*..	..9:15*...10:00...12:00...3:35*..4:00..5:10*...5:50*..					..8:15*...10:15*..11:30*...12:25*
Sunday	6:50*..	8:00*..	..10:10*...10:00...12:30...3:35*..4:00..5:10*...5:50*..					..8:15*...10:15*..11:30*...12:25*
Holiday	6:50*..	8:00*..	..10:10*...10:00...12:00...3:35*..4:00..5:10*...5:50*..					..8:15*...10:15*..11:30*...12:25*

	A. M.		Leave Alcatraz		P. M.							A. M.
Week-Day	6:35*..	7:20*...8:20...	..9:00*...11:20...12:50...3:25*..				..4:50*..5:40*..6:50..8:00*...10:00*...11:20*...12:15*
Sunday	6:35*..	7:50*..	..10:00*...11:20...1:20...3:25*..				..4:50*..5:40*..6:50..8:00*...10:00*...11:20*...12:15*
Holiday	6:35*..	7:50*..	..10:00*...11:20...12:50...3:25*..				..4:50*..5:40*..6:50..8:00*...10:00*...11:20*...12:15*

Asterisk, Launch *WARDEN JOHNSTON*   No Asterisk, Steamer *COXE*

U.S.P. Alcatraz 8 6-29-45 500

Children and wives of correctional officers lived in a close-knit community on Alcatraz, where commuting by boat to school or work on the mainland was part of everyday island life.

§

The Island Becomes a National Park

IN JULY 1964, THE BUREAU OF PRISONS transferred care
of the empty buildings on Alcatraz to the federal government's General
Services Administration (GSA). While the GSA offered the island to
various uninterested government agencies, local politicians and citizens alike argued for a new future for Alcatraz. San Francisco Mayor
George Christopher suggested placing a western sister of the Statue of
Liberty on the island. Other proposals were debated in the press. A
presidential commission decided that Alcatraz should be the site of a
memorial to the United Nations, founded in San Francisco in 1945.
None of the proposals ever amounted to anything, however, and without an interested federal taker, the GSA declared the island "surplus
government property" in May 1964, prior to putting it on the auction
block. When Mayor Joseph Alioto announced that San Francisco
wanted to acquire Alcatraz, the GSA gave him a few months to prepare
a plan for the island.

Alioto's call for proposals brought in hundreds of new
ideas, including theme parks, cultural centers, a bird sanctuary and
ideas for commercial use. The mayor finally accepted the proposal sub-
mitted by Texas oil millionaire Lamar Hunt, which called for demolish-
ing nearly every structure on the rock and making it a commercial site.
Outraged citizens beseeched the Department of the Interior to make
the island part of the National Park System, and a quick study by the
National Park Service in the fall of 1969 revealed that Alcatraz offered
a "matchless opportunity" for a national park.

The Indian Occupation

The future of Alcatraz Island was put on hold, however,
when Native Americans and other activists seized the island on
November 20, 1969. Thus began the "Indian Occupation" of Alcatraz,
a 19-month event that sought to focus the nation's attention on the
plight of Native Americans and to create a Native American Cultural
Center and University. The occupation picked up support from a variety of sources, but negotiations between the Native Americans and the
government dragged on for months. The dream of those occupying the

Graffiti bears silent testi-
mony to the Native
American occupation of
Alcatraz in 1969–1971.

island, many of them families, members of religious orders, celebrities and local university students imbued with the same idealism and passion for cultural reforms that were sweeping local campuses, died in internal squabbling and government intransigence in March 1970.

 During the occupation, Alcatraz was vandalized—almost every window on the island was broken, electrical wires were stripped for scrap, and lights were shattered. On June 1, 1970, fires broke out that destroyed the lighthouse keepers' quarters, the warden's house (formerly the residence of the military commandant), the prison doctor's home built in the 1880s, and the social hall. On June 11, 1971, federal marshals landed on the island and removed the last 15 occupiers. However, the events on Alcatraz had electrified the nation and the island's occupation was a turning point for the Native American movement. "Alcatraz Is Not an Island," proclaimed the first occupiers. Indeed, it had become a powerful symbol of Indian rights.

 After the Native Americans were removed, the GSA once again took charge of the vacant island. To ensure that it would never again be occupied, the GSA demolished living quarters on Alcatraz. Concrete apartment houses on the parade ground became piles of rubble.

 The destruction of the buildings galvanized public support to do something positive about Alcatraz. At the same time, the National Park Service, interested in the island since 1969, was creating a much larger park in the San Francisco Bay area designed to fend off the encroaching development on the city's western shores and the Marin Headlands across the Bay. The result, signed into law on October 27, 1972, was the Golden Gate National Recreation Area—a new, expansive urban national park. Alcatraz Island's 22 acres became part of the Recreation Area.

Salamanders
A small population of California slender salamanders lives on the parade ground and near the eastern side of Alcatraz.

Opening the Island

 When Alcatraz opened for public tours in 1973, its buildings stood open to the rain and fog. The shells of the burned-out warden's house, lighthouse keepers' quarters and officers' club, the broken windows, lack of electricity or running water, and an unkempt appearance had altered the industrial landscape of the island. Graffiti marked the walls of nearly every structure, and piles of moldering clothes and papers left from the penitentiary and the Native American occupation littered vacant rooms. After years of neglect, the gardens once tended by soldiers and prison inmates had run wild and gradually claimed much of the island.

 The continual erosion of Alcatraz's northwestern shore collapsed the roadway leading past the prison laundry, and the salt air had eaten away at rusting metal. A massive steel catwalk and tower that linked the Model Industries Building to the recreation yard had collapsed, and the catwalk outside the prison dining hall was removed before its rusting supports gave way and fell on passing visitors. Grass

Brown Pelicans
Once driven nearly to extinction by DDT and other shell-weakening poisons, brown pelicans are beginning to recover, and are occasionally seen perching on pilings or rocks on Alcatraz.

sprouted in the cracked concrete roads, and flowers ran wild, choking the gardens and spreading down hillsides, over crumbling rock, and onto the bare rubble of the parade ground.

Rangers guided visitors on walks around the island and through the cellhouse. The National Park Service installed a generator on the dock to bring electricity to the island, and shipped in bottles of fresh water. They concentrated their restoration work on the cellhouse and built a museum and bookstore within the brick casements of Building 64.

The rest of Alcatraz was left undisturbed save for occasional visits by rangers or Park Service planners, historians, and naturalists. Birds returned to Alcatraz. Gull colonies thrived on the cellhouse roof and along the closed perimeter of the island.

In 1980, National Park Service naturalists began to study Alcatraz's flora and fauna, and ongoing fieldwork continues to examine and record the island's inhabitants.

Tidepools

Sea life once abounded on Alcatraz. "In early days it was the resort of seals and sea lions, and was white with the deposit of these animals and birds," wrote oceanographer George Davidson in 1889. Even now, harbor seals and sea lions occasionally visit the island's shores, beaching on the rocks and tidepools.

But today, they come ashore on the plateau of broken rock and debris that rings Alcatraz, the result of more than a century of human efforts to shape the island. Irregularly shaped and tumbled, the debris forms the only manmade tidepools on San Francisco Bay.

Starfish, top and sea anemones, above, thrive in the tidepools ringing Alcatraz.

Alcatraz owes its present shape to the Army's fortification of "the Rock" in the 1850s, '60s, and '70s. When the mounded slopes of the island were blasted to form steep walls and a plateau for gun emplacements, the Army cast the debris into the ocean. Mixed with the tons of rock is rubble from every building that once stood on Alcatraz. The 22-acre island has few places to bury or dispose of demolished buildings, or other debris, for that matter.

Nearly everything taken to Alcatraz is either still there, lying mixed with the rocks that form the tidepools, or resting in the water off the island's shores. Huge pieces of granite, brick and concrete from military fortifications and other buildings, parts of cast-iron cannon carriages, pieces of steam machinery from the 19th-century fog signals, truck and automobile frames and engine blocks, and fence posts, chain-link and barbed wire from the penitentiary, all lie in the shallows. The brittle, bright-red rust of metal mixes with the dark green of corroded brass and copper.

Amid the manmade debris, nudibranchs and other sea life add living color to the tidepools, and offer a source of food for many of the seabirds living on the island.

The Birds of Alcatraz

Birds have always been a part of Alcatraz. Named by Spanish explorers for its seabirds, Alcatraz was called " Bird Island" by early San Francisco settlers.

Once disturbed by human residents, birds have now returned to Alcatraz in large numbers. Field rangers note 108 different species that have adopted this abandoned cultural landscape, including 18 that breed here, 20 that stop by seasonally, and 73 that visit occasionally.

Distinguished from other herons by their black "caps" and heads, black-crowned night-herons seem to be thriving on Alcatraz. Shy by day, at night these small birds quietly stalk fishes and other food in shallow water.

A diverse collection of birds inhabit Alcatraz. Some 600 western gulls live on the cliffs, on the parade ground, and atop the buildings on Alcatraz, forming the third largest western gull colony on the northern California coast. Making up 15 percent of the Bay Area's gull population, these birds fill the air with their calls year-round. The population peaks between January and April, however, during the early breeding season. In 1990, naturalists counted nearly 500 nests on the island. The gulls feed on fish (usually anchovies), worms, insects, and small rodents, such as the deer mice inhabiting the rubble piles on the parade ground. They also pick up mussels, crabs, snails, and even sea stars in the tidepools, or scavenge garbage.

Black-crowned night-herons also breed on Alcatraz, establishing nests in mid-February each year. Their young hatch in April, although some adult birds continue to lay clutches of eggs throughout the spring and early summer. Biologists counted 168 nests on Alcatraz in 1990, which represents nearly 10 percent of the Bay Area's population of these nocturnal feeders. Isolated Alcatraz is a safe haven for

Telling Cormorants Apart

Three different species of cormorants can be seen sunning on the island's cliffs and rocks, wings spread to dry in the wind. The pelagic cormorant, a small, 24- to 30-inch-long bird, is all black, with a red pouch under its bill. When the sunlight hits its feathers in flight, the pelagic cormorant takes on a green gloss, and you can see white patches on the sides of breeding birds. The slightly larger Brandt's cormorant is a dark bird with a band around its pouch that becomes bright blue in the breeding season. Double-crested cormorants are also black, but have a patch of bare orange skin under their bills. White tufts of feathers curve behind each eye of a breeding adult.

The Western Gull

The most common bird on Alcatraz, nearly 500 western gulls nest here in early summer. A large bird, ranging from 24- to 27-inches long with a 58-inch wing span, the western gull is snowy white with a dark gray back and wings, a yellow bill with a red spot near the tip, and pink legs. Immature birds are dark gray-brown, and won't resemble the adults until they're four years old.

The gulls on Alcatraz represent a re-established colony that had been devastated by egg collecting during the California Gold Rush. This colony is part of a large population of gulls in the Bay region that includes nearly 25,000 living on the Farallon Islands in the Pacific Ocean.

these birds, many of which are now accustomed to human visitors and nest next to well-traveled pathways.

Other birds breed on the island, including ravens, white-crowned sparrows, song sparrows, brown-headed cowbirds, pelagic and Brandt's cormorants, mallards, and pigeon guillemots, which inhabit the bare rock ledges and cliffs of Alcatraz. Eight other species of birds remain on the island year-round. Among them are rock doves, mourning doves, Anna's hummingbirds, Allen's hummingbirds, barn swallows, European starlings, and house finches. As this diversity of birds attests, the island serves as a transitional point between seabirds and land birds.

Alcatraz is also a refuge for birds who rest and feed in San Francisco Bay and surrounding waters. Thousands of seabirds can sometimes be seen floating on swells rolling in through the Golden Gate. Many stop at Alcatraz before moving on.

Brown pelicans and the peregrine falcon, both federally protected endangered species, visit Alcatraz Island. Heermann's gulls attempted to nest on the Island in 1981 and 1983, the first time this species was observed nesting north of the Mexican border. Loons use the island's offshore territory—as many as 150 red-throated and common loons can be spotted at certain times of year.

Breeding activity among the birds on Alcatraz peaks between January and July each year. To protect the nesting birds, the National Park Service regulates visitor access to certain areas of the island during the breeding season.

The Future of Alcatraz

Future plans for Alcatraz call for controlled access to all of the island along a perimeter trail and restoration and rehabilitation of certain buildings. The National Park Service hopes to expand public access to include all the unique sites on Alcatraz and broaden its interpretation of the diverse natural and cultural history of the island.

Many who visit Alcatraz are probably drawn by the island's reputation as a federal penitentiary. Others want to see the unique landscape of crumbling ruins, steeped in our country's history, against the spectacular scenery of San Francisco, the Bay and the Golden Gate.

Regardless of what draws them, everyone who comes to Alcatraz leaves with a sense of the island's isolation in the midst of a bustling seaport—its fate carved by the forces of tides and currents, wind and fog, human endeavor and struggle for life on the rock.

A SAMPLING OF SPECIES ON ALCATRAZ ISLAND

Plants
Agave *Agave americana*
California blackberry *Rubus vitifolius*
California poppy *Eschscholzia californica*
Coyote brush *Baccharis pilularis*
Eucalyptus *Eucalyptus globulus*
Mirror plant *Coprosma repens*
Monterey cypress *Cupressus macrocarpa*
Rose *Rosa* spp.

Amphibians & Reptiles
California slender salamander *Batrachoseps attenuatus*

Birds
Anna's hummingbird *Calypte anna*
Allen's hummingbird *Selasphorus sasin*
Barn swallow *Hirundo rustica*
Black-crowned night-heron *Nycticorax nycticorax*
Black phoebe *Sayornis nigricans*
Brandt's cormorant *Phalacrocorax penicillatus*
Brown-headed cowbird *Molothrus ater*
Brown pelican *Pelecanus occidentalis*
Common loon *Gavia immer*
Double-crested cormorant *Phalacrocorax auritus*
European starling *Sturnus vulgaris*
Heermann's gull *Larus heermanni*
House finch *Carpodacus mexicanus*
Mallard *Anas platyrhynchos*
Mourning dove *Zenaida macroura*
Pelagic cormorant *Phalacrocorax pelagicus*
Peregrine falcon *Falco peregrinus*
Pigeon guillemot *Cepphus columba*
Raven *Corvus corax*
Red-throated loon *Gavia stellata*
Rock dove *Columba livia*
Song sparrow *Melospiza melodia*
Western gull *Larus occidentalis*
White-crowned sparrow *Zonotrichia leucophrys*

Mammals
Deer mouse *Peromyscus maniculatus*

About Alcatraz Island

Alcatraz is open every day except Christmas and New Years' Day, from the first to last ferry departure from Pier 41 at Fisherman's Wharf.

How to Get There
Transportation to Alcatraz is via ferryboats, departing from Pier 41 at Fisherman's Wharf. The ferry trip lasts ten minutes. A round-trip visit takes between two and three hours. Advance ticket purchases are essential in the busy summer season. Call (415) 546-7805 for ferry service information.

What to See and Do
Rangers lead a variety of guided tours of the island, or you can walk around on your own with the self-guiding trail brochure or the *Official Map and Guide to Alcatraz*. You'll find it at all Park bookstores.

Take an award-winning self-guiding audio-cassette tour of the cellhouse, available in six languages at the cellhouse entrance for a nominal fee. All voices on this tour are those of actual inmates or correctional officers who lived on Alcatraz.

Tour exhibits, including "Alcatraz and the American Prison Experience," and see an historical slide show in the barracks building just above the Alcatraz ferry landing.

Walk around the island for breathtaking views of San Francisco Bay and the city. The most spectacular views are from the lighthouse plaza and the west walkway. Be prepared for steep climbs. No wheelchairs are available on the Island, however the island and cellhouse are accessible. Hills are steep, so assistance may be required. Pets are not allowed on the island except for seeing-eye dogs. Bring water. The island's supply of drinking water is limited.

What to wear:
Dress warmly and wear comfortable walking shoes. Alcatraz lies directly in the path of cold wind and fog sweeping through the Golden Gate.

Suggested Reading
Babyak, Jolene. EYEWITNESS ON ALCATRAZ: INTERVIEWS OF GUARDS, FAMILIES AND PRISONERS WHO LIVED ON THE ROCK. Berkeley: Ariel Vamp Press, 1988.

Johnston, James A. ALCATRAZ ISLAND PRISON AND THE MEN WHO LIVE THERE. New York: Charles A. Scribner, 1949.

Quillen, James. ALCATRAZ FROM INSIDE: THE HARD YEARS, 1942-1952. San Francisco: Golden Gate National Park Association, 1991.

Martini, John A. FORTRESS ALCATRAZ: GUARDIAN OF THE GOLDEN GATE. Kailua, Hawaii: Pacific Monograph, 1991.

Thompson, E. N. THE ROCK: A HISTORY OF ALCATRAZ ISLAND 1847-1972. Historic Resource Study, Golden Gate National Recreational Area, California. U.S. Department of the Interior, National Park Service, Historic Preservation Division, Denver, 1979.

About the Author

James P. Delgado is executive director of the Vancouver Maritime Museum in British Columbia. Formerly the historian of the Golden Gate National Recreation Area and chief maritime historian of the National Park Service, he is the author of several books. This is his second book about Alcatraz.

The Golden Gate National Park Association wishes to thank the staff of the Golden Gate National Recreation Area who helped review and produce this publication.

GGNPA Production Management
Charles Money
Greg Moore

Editor
Nora L. Deans

Design
Nancy E. Koc

Photography
All photographs by Roy Eisenhardt except:

Bancroft Library, UC Berkeley (pages 9, 11, 15, 18)
Maritime Museum Archives (pages 11, 14, 18, 21, 31, 33, 35, 37)
David Tise (page 36)

Illustrations
Megan Englander, courtesy of Marin Museum Society, Inc (page 8)
Karen Montgomery (page 7)
Lawrence Ormsby (pages 1, 3, 6, 18, 41-top, 43, 44)
Claus Sievert (pages 10, 13, 40, 41-bottom)

Set in Sabon Antiqua on an Apple Macintosh with Quark Express 3.0

Printed in Hong Kong on recycled paper